For

Compiled by Helen H. Moore

Illustrated by Amy Dietrich

PETER PAUPER PRESS, INC.
WHITE PLAINS, NEW YORK

To my sister, Patricia Moore Schmidt,
who has not only been there, and done that—
she's got the T-shirt

Book design by Mullen & Katz

202 Mamaroneck Avenue
White Plains, NY 10601

ISBN 0-88088-103-8
Printed in China
7 6 5 4 3 2 1

Been There, Done That

Advice from Women in the Know

Contents

Introduction

We have more options, and more of a voice in defining our own destiny, than ever before in history. Work, family, success, relationships, spirituality—everything that defines us as human, as women—is changing. It's an exhilarating time—but it can also be a stressful one.

That life today presents us with an unprecedented array of choices is a two-edged sword. Sometimes it's hard to know which choice of the many spread before us is the right one. That's when it helps to have the counsel of those trailblazers who have already passed our way. That's what this book is all about. *Advice from Women in the Know. . .* for women on their way up in the world.

Advising a modern woman isn't easy. We're strong-minded, and the high expectations we place on ourselves make us demand more from those who would presume to give us advice. Simple-minded solutions are *out.* We want to know what worked for the women we look up to, but, ultimately, we trust ourselves to do what feels right. The women we admire are leaders, not followers. In allowing ourselves to be advised by them, we are learning from the best.

The women quoted in this book run with the wolves, swim with the sharks, and even, in some cases, "float like a butterfly, sting like a bee." Some are poets, some are philosophers, some are jesters, some are fighters, but all are women who have *been there, done that,* and have valuable information to impart about what they've learned along the way.

H. H. M.

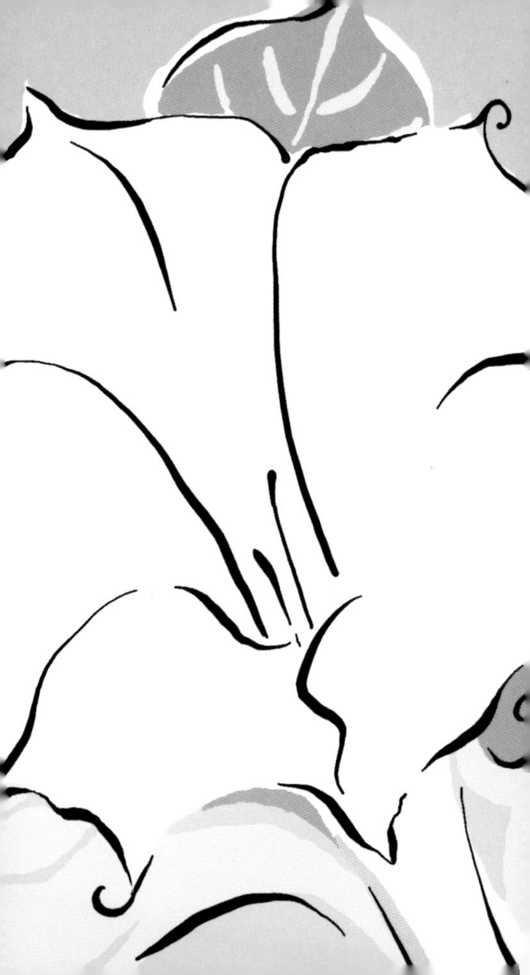

Know Thyself

Love is what we are born with. Fear is what we learn. . . . Love is the essential reality and our purpose on earth. . . . Meaning does not lie in things. Meaning lies in us.

Marianne Williamson,
A Return to Love

I've learned to trust myself, to listen to truth, to not be afraid of it, and to not try and hide it.

Sarah McLachlan

Ultimately, all women, to feel truly fulfilled, must throughout a lifetime integrate the many facets of their personalities, and each woman must do so in her own unique and individual way.

Dr. Toni Grant

You can't be afraid to deal
with your demons.

Lucinda Williams

Empowering yourself and clinging to the things that are sacred about being a woman are what gives you power as a female. I think you shouldn't have to change who you are to compete or to be treated equally.

Sheryl Crow

Both women and men need to confront the divine madness in themselves and to differentiate it from destructive craziness on both the individual and the social level.

Linda Schierse Leonard

In a lifetime, I think everyone sinks to the pits. If you've been to the bottom, you have an opportunity to be a more compassionate person.

Joni Mitchell

I'm true to myself, and I always try to do the right things. I've always said my prayers and they've been reciprocated.

Queen Latifah

Don't compromise yourself. You're all you've got.

Janis Joplin

You'll never find yourself until you face the truth.

Pearl Bailey

"Love Your Neighbor as Yourself" Means First You Have to Love Yourself

Dress loosely, take a great deal of exercise, be particular about your diet and sleep enough. The body has great influence upon the mind.

Elizabeth Cady Stanton

You have to stay in shape. My grandmother, she started walking five miles a day when she was 60. She's 97 today and we don't know *where* she is.

Ellen DeGeneres

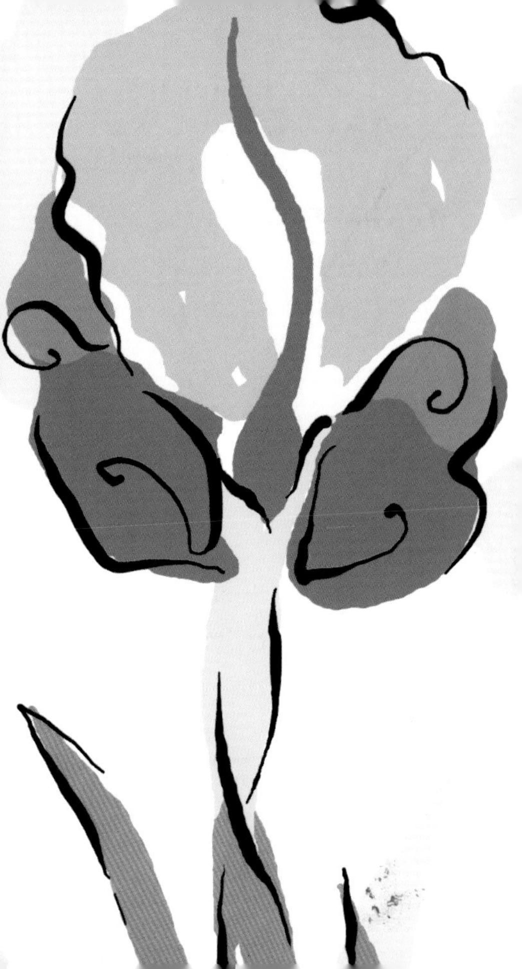

You learn to accept that one day you'll be famous, the next day infamous. One day you'll be rich, the next day poor. One day people will think you're great, the next day they'll think you're terrible. And this is just the stuff of life.

Alice Walker

I don't think that I was sent down here to get robbed.

Ashley Judd

One of the secrets of a happy life is continuous small treats.

Iris Murdoch

I Enjoy Being a Girrrrrrlll

This is the female era.

Missy Misdemeanor Elliot

What I have to say is far more important than how long my eyelashes are.

Alanis Morissette

It is time to reinvent our understanding of adolescence so that young women can combine their voices at an earlier time to bring the remarkable gifts of the feminine into a world that has never needed them more.

Joan Borysenko

I like getting dressed up, because it's kind of like getting married every time you do it. I'm very girly that way.

Julia Louis-Dreyfus

I'm completely behind women dressing up and looking as good as they can. I could go out in a gray frump's frock, but I suit orange much better than I suit gray.

Elizabeth Hurley

Fashion is something that goes in one year and out the other.

Anonymous

I really like the fact that people see me
and say, "Oh, she has a great body.
She must be an athlete."

Cynthia Cooper

Women are intimidated by triathlons.
But when they see I'm just like them
and not some big huge Amazon,
it makes a difference.
They say to themselves,
"Wow. Maybe I can do this, too."
And they can.

Heather Fuhr

Feminism's agenda is basic:
It asks that women not be forced
to "choose" between public justice
and private happiness.

Susan Faludi

It's impossible to be a woman and not be political.

Roseanne

Sisterhood is very important. That hood is a covering. Sisters make everything possible on this earth.

Sonia Sanchez

I find it nothing short of obscene that women are forced to expose ourselves to politicians—forced to submit our private matters, our private decisions . . . to public debate! Men's reproduction isn't regulated by the state—and it shouldn't be. Neither should women's.

Faye Wattleton

There are no rules for single women,
so we are able to make our own.

Merle Shain

I am a woman's woman.
I love hanging out with women.

Lucy Lawless

Oh, God, I love being a girl—
a "human girl person."

Laura Dern

When Times Get Tough

Go back to when you were ten and try to remember what kind of a girl you were. It's still there, it doesn't go away, get it back. You were brave, you were so brave.

Nancy Friday

Action is the antidote to despair.

Joan Baez

Advice is what we ask for when we already know the answer but wish we didn't.

Erica Jong

When all else fails and I just want to lock myself in the house and stuff chocolate into my mouth, I remember that I live on a planet that is part of a galaxy that is in an infinite universe. Gives you some perspective.

Gabrielle Reece

Once in a while, if you pay close attention, people will come into your life who will help to lift you out of the dark place you're in, and give you the opportunity to change.

Gillian Anderson

As you have new experiences—new pain and new joy—what came before begins to fade into the background. It's there if you want to look at it, but what's right in front of you is really what's important.

Holly Palmer

Remember, Ginger Rogers did everything Fred Astaire did, but she did it backwards and in high heels.

Faith Whittlesey

And I think that's important, to know how the water's gone over the dam before you start to describe it. It helps to have been over the dam yourself.

E. Annie Proulx

Women in Love, out of Love, on Love . . .

Love is a fruit in season at all times, and within reach of every hand.

Mother Teresa

If it is your time, love will track you down like a cruise missile.

Lynda Barry

Men fascinate and bewilder me.

Roseanne Cash

Never judge someone
by who he's in love with;
judge him by his friends. People fall in
love with the most appalling people.
Take a cool, appraising
glance at his pals.
Cynthia Heimel

If a man wants to treat you
very special, let him.
Neve Campbell

If grass can grow through cement, love
can find you at every time in your life.
Cher

Love is like pi: natural, irrational,
and very important.
Lisa Hoffman

Dating's frightening, I think, for anybody. I've been very fortunate. I've had few and far between, but that's just because I wait and find somebody that's been a friend.

Sandra Bullock

I really don't care about going anywhere fancy or expensive. But I love it when people put thought into [a date]. The dinner-and-a-movie idea is boring to me. I'm more like, "Hey, I'll pick you up and we'll go have a picnic at the beach."

Danielle Fishel

Be careful of wigs.

Spoken by Patsy,
Absolutely Fabulous
BBC television program

I'm a sucker for romance.
Movies are so good at romance.
And romance is a great part of all our lives. Love—or else the lack of love—is felt so deeply by all of us.

Meg Ryan

I think probably all your romances happen so you can understand the right person when he comes into your life.

Salma Hayek

Then Comes Marriage . . .

It is always incomprehensible to a man
that a woman should ever refuse an
offer of marriage.

Jane Austen

Be aware that there is very little
bargaining power in a prenuptial
negotiation: The party willing to
walk away from the marriage
has the upper hand.

Ivana Trump

I love being married.
It's so great to find that one special
person you want to annoy
for the rest of your life.

Rita Rudner

I'm a big believer in marriage.
I married in my 20s; I married in my
30s; and I married—well,
you get the idea.

Mary Matalin

In negotiating with rejected lovers or
husbands, women must stop thinking
they can make everyone happy.

Camille Paglia

With all heart-sore lovers I say,
"I don't know what went wrong."
But I suspect it was the house.

Maya Angelou

There is always something left to love.
And if you ain't learned that, you ain't
learned nothing.

Lorraine Hansberry

Keeping Up Appearances

Just because we're young doesn't mean it's too soon to start fighting gravity.

Joyce Maynard,
To Die For

Normal is in the eye of the beholder.

Whoopi Goldberg

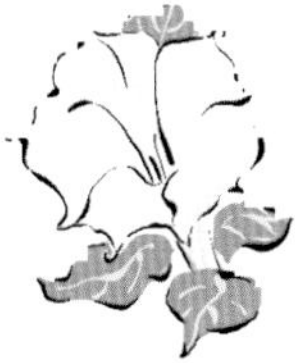

Don't tolerate me as different. Accept me as part of the spectrum of normalcy.

Ann Northrop

Beauty Comes from Within

A happy heart comes first,
then the happy face.
Shania Twain

Holding on to anger
only gives you tense muscles.
Joan Lunden

The day you become addiction-free
is a day of great liberation.
Chrissie Hynde

A habit is hell for those you love.
Billie Holiday

Way to Go

Where I was born and where and how I have lived is unimportant. It is what I have done with where I have been that should be of interest.

Georgia O'Keeffe

The way I see it, if you want the rainbow, you gotta put up with the rain.

Dolly Parton

I'm learning that if you want something, you prioritize—that's just what you have to do.

Jenna Elfman

If there's a book you want to read
but it hasn't been written yet,
then you must write it.
Toni Morrison

Obstacles are those frightful things
you see when you take your eyes
off the goal.
Hannah Moore

Whoever handles the chaos wins.
Marion Jones

I believe in luck if you give it
plenty of help.
Rumer Godden

The wider your span of control,
the greater your power.
Harriet Rubin

In order to achieve my goals,
I had to treat the people I worked with
as if we were all part of a team.
I had to give them responsibilities,
and then trust them to fulfill them.
Heather Whitestone,
Miss America 1996

America promises you nothing.
America is what you promise yourself.
Ruquiayah Brown

For economic health, and to get women used to discussing money, forming an investment club, even if the amount of stock is minuscule, is a good idea.
Naomi Wolf

For me it's the challenge—the challenge to try to beat myself or do better than I did in the past. I try to keep in mind not what I have accomplished but what I have to try to accomplish in the future.
Jackie Joyner-Kersee

F-e-e-e-e-e-l-i-n-g-s!

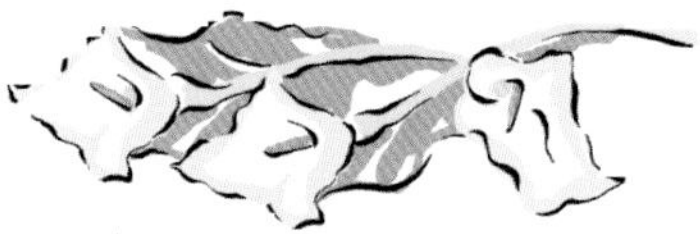

Each of us wages a private battle each day between the grand fantasies we have for ourselves and what actually happens.

Cathy Guisewite

Anger often leaves us so rattle-brained and confused that it's hard to sort out the issues. Keeping a daily anger diary or journal is one way to work these issues through.

Sandra Thomas

Man invented language to satisfy his deep need to complain.

Lily Tomlin

Now that we've broken the barriers
that once kept us out of law schools
and board rooms, we have unearthed
another, more hidden source of many
of our limitations: the human heart.

Elizabeth Mitchell

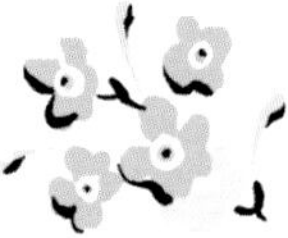

I've got enough guilt to
start my own religion.

Tori Amos

I've been there and all I can say is
at the end of the day, money and fame
don't bring you happiness.

Rene Russo

Isolation is aloneness that feels
forced upon you, like a punishment.
Solitude is aloneness you choose
and embrace. I think great things
can come out of solitude,
out of going to a place where
all is quiet except the beating
of your heart.

Jeanne Marie Laskas

It's also very common for women
to experience sadness, tearfulness,
anxiety, irritability, anger, and
mood swings after childbirth. . . .
Help is available and should be
sought right away. . . . Make sure
that you get the care and attention
you deserve.

Lauren Hartman

I hate ticks. Anything that embeds himself beneath your skin is not okay with me. Like that Cole Porter song, "I've Got You Under My Skin"? Well, I don't want you under my skin, how about that?

Drew Barrymore

The last part of the word *jealousy* is "lousy," because that's how you feel.

Alisha Fernandez

I know I grew up very naive and sheltered, but I like that. I feel sad when I see kids who have experienced too much too young. I'm glad I could wait this long before I had to deal with reality.

Katie Holmes

I learned that basics are
very important. I learned respect,
good listening skills and how to
defend myself. But the
most important thing I gained
was confidence.

Bridgett Riley

Woman of the World

Today, what we share is more
important than what sets us apart
from one another.
What we have in common is
infinitely more important than
what divides us.
Anne Rice

The gradual integration of the world
has led to an interlocking of interests
that is inexorably driving humanity
toward greater unity and cooperation.
Charlotte Saikowski

Hope for the earth lies not with
leaders but in your own heart and soul.
If you decide to save the earth,
it will be saved.

Helen Caldicott

The truest expression of a people
is its dances and its music.
Bodies never lie.

Agnes de Mille

We can say "Peace on Earth,"
we can sing about it, preach about it
or pray about it, but if we have not
internalized the mythology to
make it happen inside us,
then it will not be.

Betty Shabazz

It just seems like as an artist,
you can excuse a lot of things because
you created something that was
meaningful to the culture.
And my argument has always been no,
you have to live a good life,
be a good person.

Natalie Merchant

The universe is made up of stories,
not atoms.

Muriel Rukeyser

Nature provides exceptions
to every rule.

Margaret Fuller

As a woman, I have no country.
As a woman my country is the world.
Virginia Woolf

Don't shut yourself up in a bandbox
because you are a woman, but
understand what is going on,
and educate yourself to take part
in the world's work for it all affects
you and yours.
Louisa May Alcott

The Spirited Woman

Trying to live in a way that allows
you to perceive the spiritual dimension
of everyday life is, for me,
something essential.

Joan Osborne

Listening to a child or teenager.
Don't try to tell them anything,
just listen.

Sarah Van Gelder,
*suggestion for learning how to
live a meaningful life*

What is truly sacred is free of all
our definitions, conceptualizations,
and limitations.

Gangaji

Trying to use another language.
Walking in the woods.
Dancing to reggae.
Cooking vegetables just pulled
from your garden.
Ice skating.
Smelling wood fire.
Eating olives.
Listening to friends tell stories
of their lives.
Whistling.

Susan Griffin,
suggestion for learning how to live a meaningful life

We can spout a lot of words, but I think really it's our actions that determine the meaning of our lives.

Paula Cole

When you aren't provided with tools
by your family or culture—or were
provided with tools that didn't work—
you have to invent new ones.

Sylvia Boorstein

No pessimist ever discovered the
secrets of the stars or sailed to an
uncharted land or opened a new
heaven to the human spirit.

Helen Keller

Honey, everyone gets to
decide their own fate to a certain
degree. And to another degree,
it's not in your hands.
And I trust in that.

Angela Bassett

Only in growth, reform
and change, paradoxically enough,
is true security to be found.

Anne Morrow Lindbergh

It is not that we *have* a soul,
we *are* a soul.

Amelia E. Barr

Believe it or not, something good in life can come out of something bad. For me, it was my music.

Robyn

Adventure is worthwhile in itself.

Amelia Earhart

Nothing in life is to be feared, it is only to be understood.

Marie Curie

Family Style

Round parents have square kids.
Winona Ryder

A mother is not a person to lean on but a person to make leaning unnecessary.
Dorothy Canfield Fisher

Anything that changes you emotionally changes your work, and being a parent has definitely deepened my emotions.
Nicole Kidman

When love is gone, there's always justice. And when justice is gone, there's always force. And when force is gone, there's always Mom. Hi, Mom!
Laurie Anderson

Divas and How to Be One

I don't mean to be a diva, but some days you wake up and you're Barbra Streisand.

Courtney Love

I hadda be great. I couldn't be medium. My mouth was too big.

Barbra Streisand

I just go where the light is glittering, and pretty much do what would enchant me.

Bette Midler

A long, long time ago I decided
I was going to have a kind of mystical
presence, so I made my clothes,
my boots, my hair, and my whole
being go with that. . . . I've always
believed in good witches—not bad
witches—and fairies and angels.

Stevie Nicks

But like my mother said,
I studied acting, I studied dancing,
I studied singing, I was prepared.
And that's, uh, the real message.
Which is be prepared.

Goldie Hawn

Friends and Memories

The most wonderfully complex
fictional character is much less
complicated than the most
boring actual person.
Elizabeth McCracken

To send a letter is a good way to
go somewhere without moving
anything but your heart.
Phyllis Theroux

It seems to me that trying to live
without friends is like milking a bear
to get cream for your morning coffee.
It is a whole lot of trouble, and then
not worth much after you get it.
Zora Neale Hurston

The past, with its pleasure,
its rewards, its foolishness,
its punishments, is there for each
of us forever,
and it should be.

Lillian Hellman

Life isn't a matter of milestones,
but of moments.

Rose Kennedy

Some memories are realities,
and are better than anything that can
ever happen to one again.

Willa Cather

A Girl's Gotta Have a Sense of Humor

If you reside in a state where you attain your legal majority while still in your teens, pretend that you don't. There isn't an adult alive who would want to be contractually bound by a decision he came to at the age of 19.

Fran Lebowitz

My mother always told me I wouldn't amount to anything because I procrastinate. I said "Just wait."

Judy Tenuta

The statistics on sanity are that one out of every four Americans is suffering from some form of mental illness. Think of your three best friends. If they're okay, then it's you.

Rita Mae Brown

Normal is not something to aspire to, it's something to get away from.

Jodie Foster

A sobering thought:
What if, at this very moment,
I *am* living up to my full potential?

Jane Wagner

And in the End . . .

It is only possible to live happily ever after on a day-to-day basis.

Margaret Bonnano